GOOD GRIEF, IT'S YOUR BIRTHDAY!

Artwork by
Charles M. Schulz

HARVEST HOUSE PUBLISHERS

EUGENE, OREGON

GOOD GRIEF, IT'S YOUR BIRTHDAY!

Copyright © 2006 by Harvest House Publishers
Eugene, Oregon 97402

ISBN-13: 978-0-7369-1522-9
ISBN-10: 0-7369-1522-2

Product #: 6915222

PEANUTS © United Feature Syndicate, Inc.

All works of art reproduced in this book are copyrighted by Charles Schulz and may not be reproduced without permission. For more information regarding art prints featured in this book, please contact:

United Media Licensing
200 Madison Avenue, 4th Floor
New York, New York 10016
www.unitedmedialicensing.com

Design and production by Garborg Design Works, Savage, Minnesota

Harvest House Publishers has made every effort to trace the ownership of all poems and quotes. In the event of a question arising from the use of a poem or quote, we regret any error made and will be pleased to make the necessary correction in future editions of this book.

Printed in China

06 07 08 09 10 11 12 13/ LP / 10 9 8 7 6 5 4 3 2 1

TO

FROM

3

Remember, the greatest gift is not found in a store
nor under a tree, but in the hearts of true friends.

CINDY LEW

> But after all, what are birthdays? Here today and gone tomorrow...
>
> A.A. MILNE

Every gift, though it be small, is in reality great if given with affection.

PINDAR

5

The secret of staying young is to live honestly, eat slowly, and lie about your age.

A diplomat is a man who always remembers a woman's birthday but never remembers her age.

I'M SURE I'M GOING TO BE HAPPY,
AND HAVE EVERYTHING GO JUST RIGHT
FOR ME ALL THE DAYS OF MY LIFE!

LUCY

7

"Mother," said Barnaby, looking at her steadfastly as she sat down beside him…"is today my birthday?"

"Today?" she answered. "Don't you recollect it was but a week or so ago, and that summer, autumn, and winter have to pass before it comes again?"

"I remember that it has been so till now," said Barnaby. "But I think today must be my birthday too, for all that."

CHARLES DICKENS, from *Barnaby Rudge*

I DON'T KNOW WHEN MY BIRTHDAY IS, AND I DON'T KNOW HOW OLD I AM..

AND THE DAISY HILL PUPPY FARM ISN'T THERE ANYMORE! EVERYTHING'S GONE!

By the time you're eighty years old you've learned
everything. You only have to remember it.

GEORGE BURNS

Everyday is a gift, that's
why they call it a present.

AUTHOR UNKNOWN

Youth would be an
ideal state if it came a
little later in life.

HERBERT HENRY ASQUITH

*While we may
not be able to
control all that
happens to us, we
can control what
happens inside us.*

BEN FRANKLIN

LIFE IS GOING BY TOO FAST FOR ME... STOP THE CLOCK!

CHARLIE BROWN

Today, be aware of how you are spending your
1,440 beautiful moments, and spend them wisely.

AUTHOR UNKNOWN

Remember this—very little is needed to make a happy life.

MARCUS AURELIUS

I, my dear, was born today—
So all my jolly comrades say:
They bring me music, wreaths, and mirth,
And ask to celebrate my birth.

Matthew Prior

"This is your birthday. How dare you talk about anything else till you have been wished many happy returns of the day, Tim Linkinwater? God bless you, Tim! God bless you!"

CHARLES DICKENS,
from *Nicholas Nickleby*

Most of us can remember a time when a birthday—especially if it was one's own—brightened the world as if a second sun had risen.

ROBERT LUND

EVERYONE BRINGS SOMETHING TO THE PARTY.

SNOOPY

Do you count your birthdays thankfully?

HORACE

Wrinkles should merely indicate where smiles have been.

MARK TWAIN

Middle age is
when your age
starts to show
around your
middle.

BOB HOPE

The golden
age is
before us,
not behind us.

SAINT-SIMON

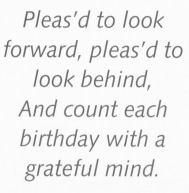

Pleas'd to look forward, pleas'd to look behind, And count each birthday with a grateful mind.

ALEXANDER POPE

Oh! how surprised their mother appeared when she was ushered out to the feast, and the full glory of the table burst upon her. Her delight in the cake was fully enough to satisfy the most exacting mind. She admired and admired it on every side, protesting that she shouldn't have supposed Polly could possibly have baked it as good in the old stove; and then she cut it, and gave a piece to every child, with a little posy on top. Wasn't it good, though! for like many other things, the cake proved better on trial than it looked, and so turned out to be really quite a good surprise all around.

MARGARET SIDNEY,
from *Five Little Peppers and How They Grew*

IT CAN'T BE
A NEW YEAR
ALREADY...I'M
NOT FINISHED
WITH LAST
YEAR!!

LUCY

MY LIFE IS LIKE A
COLORING BOOK!
EACH DAY I HAVE A
NEW PAGE WITH NEW
PICTURES TO COLOR.

RERUN

JUST REMEMBER, ONCE
YOU'RE OVER THE HILL YOU
BEGIN TO PICK UP SPEED.

CHARLES SCHULZ

Thanks to modern medical advances such as antibiotics, nasal spray, and Diet Coke, it has become routine for people in the civilized world to pass the age of 40, sometimes more than once.

DAVE BARRY

"How long did he keep his birthday?" I asked. "I never can keep *mine* more than twenty-four hours."

"Why, a birthday *stays* that long by itself!" cried Bruno. "Oo doosn't know how to keep birthdays! This Boy kept *his* a whole year!"

"And then the next birthday would begin," said Sylvie. "So it would be his birthday *always*."

"So it were," said Bruno.

LEWIS CARROLL,
from *Sylvie and Bruno*

Pa gave Laura a little wooden man he had whittled out of a stick, to be company for her rag doll, Charlotte. Ma gave her five little cakes, one for each year. Mary gave her a new dress for Charlotte. Mary had made the dress herself, when Laura thought she was sewing on her patchwork quilt…

So they went laughing to bed and lay listening to Pa and the fiddle singing. It had been a happy birthday in the little house in the Big Woods.

LAURA INGALLS WILDER

I THINK EVERY WEEK SHOULD HAVE ONE DAY IN IT WHEN BOYS GIVE PRESENTS TO GIRLS.

LUCY

There are only two ways to live your life.
One is as though nothing is a miracle.
The other is as though everything is a miracle.

ALBERT EINSTEIN

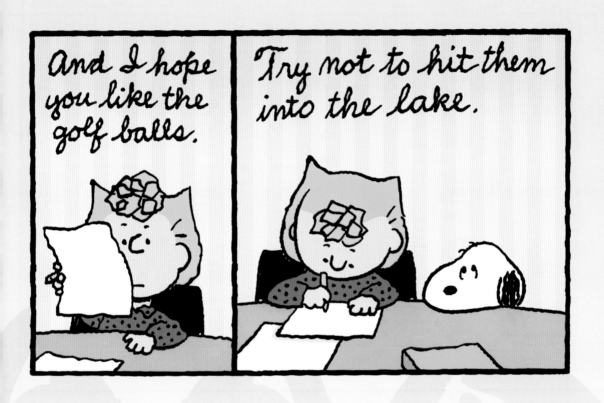

You'll find as you grow older that you weren't born such a great while ago after all. The time shortens up.

William Dean Howells

*The best way to predict
the future is to invent it.*

ALAN KAY

Thirty-five is when you
finally get your head
together and your body
starts falling apart.

CARYN LESCHEN

THE DAYS SURE GO BY IN A HURRY, DON'T THEY?

SNOOPY

Live daringly, boldly, fearlessly. Taste the relish to be found in competition—in having put forth the best within you.

HENRY J. KAISER

To me, old
age is always
15 years older
than I am.

BERNARD BARUCH

*May you live
all the days
of your life.*

JONATHAN SWIFT

33

THIS IS MY YEAR!
IT'S GOING TO BE ALL MINE!

LUCY

With mirth and laughter let old wrinkles come.

SHAKESPEARE

*You are never too old to set another
goal or to dream a new dream.*

Les Brown

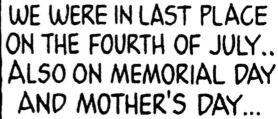

Birthdays are good for you. Statistics show that the people who have the most live the longest.

LARRY LORENZONI

The more you praise and celebrate your life,
the more there is in life to celebrate.

OPRAH WINFREY

Youth is a circumstance you can't do anything about. The trick is to grow up without getting old.

FRANK LLOYD WRIGHT

You only live once...but if you live it right, once is enough.

JOE E. LEWIS

*The best birthdays
of all are those that
haven't arrived yet.*

Robert Orben

Good judgement
comes from experience.
Sometimes, experience
comes from bad
judgement.

Christian Slater

Happiness is good health and a bad memory.

INGRID BERGMAN

Age, like distance, lends a double charm.

OLIVER HERFORD

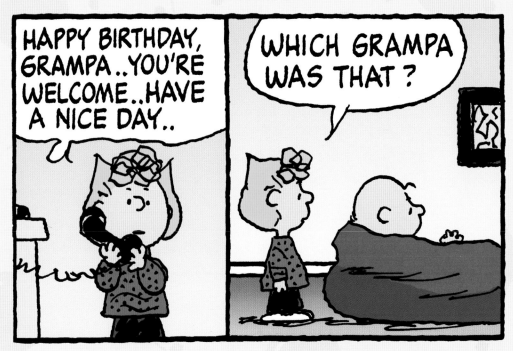

Youth is the gift of nature, but age is a work of art.

GARSON KANIN

*Our birthdays
are feathers
in the broad
wing of time.*

JEAN PAUL

Life is what happens when you're busy eating birthday cake.

Stephen Axelrod

You know you are getting old when the candles cost more than the cake.

BOB HOPE

Blowing out
candles is
good exercise
for the lungs.

AUTHOR UNKNOWN

DON'T YOU EVEN WANT TO BLOW OUT THE CANDLES?

Old age is no place for sissies.

BETTE DAVIS

THIS COULD VERY WELL BE THE MOST IMPORTANT
DAY OF YOUR LIFE!

THIS HAS BEEN A GOOD DAY!

SNOOPY